I0489982

How To Create And Dominate Your Niche

4 Simple Steps To Becoming A Market Leader

John Millar

ISBN-10:1533451753
ISBN-13:9781533451750

DEDICATION

I dedicate this book to my mother and father, who
raised me while self-employed. They
taught me to work hard and listen to everyone but to
make my own choices as to what is right
and what is wrong.. and oh, did I mention work hard?

Anyone who tells you to work smart not hard hasn't
ever done it tough and realized that if
you work smart AND hard you will achieve more than
you can possibly dream.

CONTENTS

Generating More Leads

Improve Your Sales
Conversions

Get Your Customers
Buying More Often

Increase Your Clients
Spending

GENERATE MORE LEADS

Referral System

Referrals are one of the most powerful lead generators in the world. People spreading the word are an inexpensive and very effective means of lead generation. Obviously, this can be achieved by offering exceptional value and service, but it can be further promoted by using special referral programs.

For example, you may reward someone who introduces his or her friends with a free membership or "referral" compensation, paid in the form of a gift voucher.

The key is that referrals are very valuable and you should reward those who are your best ambassadors.

Press Releases

This is where you send a newsworthy story about your business to a media outlet. However, to get the story published it must contain a newsworthy angle that is well written.

Bear in mind that journalists have to fill a certain amount of news space every day/week/month. If you make their job easy and provide them with a good story, it will be considered for publication. It is always best to call first, saying, "I am just faxing through a really good story idea." Then fax it.

In addition, follow up afterwards with another telephone call to see whether it was received. Remember, almost any business can take advantage of this form of promotion.

Post Card Mailings

Send your prospects a post card that advertises your business. This is similar to direct mail or flyers, although there are other benefits. One benefit is that postcards make for an ideal "teaser" – they do not tell you the whole story. For example, send a postcard that says, "In 2 days' time, someone will call to help double the value of your investments."

You may also like to send a post card featuring an exotic location. You could then write on the back of the post card explaining that the reader could be spending time in that very place if they take the action you want them to take. If you are using this sort of promotion, you should outline the benefits of your offer without giving too much information about the offer itself. You want to get them excited so they will look forward to hearing from you.

Named Promotional Gifts

This is where you have pens designed with your logo on them, or something similar. The gift could be as large as a set of golf clubs. Ideally, the gift should be useful and of good quality.

Window Displays

You will find people will look at displays, often because they are bored but mainly because there is no one there to pressure them. They can look for as long as they want without being harassed. This is why real estate windows work well, and always tend to attract a large number of lookers.

Do something interesting, and encourage people to come in with "More Inside!" or "Come in to try on this suit."

Listing the benefits of your product can be a great way to get your selling message across without scaring customers away. Make sure that you paint a clear picture in your prospect's mind about how much better, or easier, their life will be when they buy your goods.

This can also be an excellent opportunity for you to mention any offers or guarantees you have. Bright colours or unusual themes can also attract attention. The more people that you have looking at your window, the greater the chance of them coming inside. To create interesting window displays, consider doing a joint promotion with another company.

Host Beneficiary

This involves asking to promote your business directly to the customers of another business. There are many ways to set this up. You could offer their customers a gift voucher (and say that it is from the other business owner), offer to pay for the business owner's mail out, offer the business owner commission on any sales the strategy generates, or offer the favour in reverse.

This can work exceptionally well for almost any type of business and it is especially good when you are friends with other business people who have customers that fall into your target market.

To make it more attractive for the other business, explain that you will pay for the printing of the letters and flyers that are to be distributed. You will need to do a great sales job on the company sharing promotions with you. Many people will be suspicious and will not understand the effectiveness of this strategy in the same way that you do. Put their mind at ease by guaranteeing them you will only use soft sales techniques with their customers. You can also explain the advantage to them of how they will build greater rapport with their customers.

Internet/Web Pages

The Internet is good for virtually every type of business today, including complex products and big decision products to generate leads. People use the 'net' to research purchases and to identify potential suppliers, so a web page is absolutely necessary.

The Internet can be a major distribution channel for software, music, books, travel and other commodity type products that people do not need to touch and feel before purchasing. You can also implement cross selling on the Internet by advertising another company's products and vice versa. The Internet is also great for opening up new markets from across the country or even around the world. The cost of setting up a website versus the potential revenues is very low. A website can act as a powerful feedback tool for current customers and a way to interface with your services such as product ordering and updating account information.

Strategic Alliances

Join forces with other businesses and help each other out. You could either market yourselves under one name, making your joint business a "one-stop shop", or just have a verbal agreement to share customers, and refer them on to each other. These alliances can pay off significantly, especially if you find it difficult to get to your potential customers.

This works most effectively if the businesses involved are similar, but not competitive.

Networking Functions

These can be extremely effective. People buy from people they like, know and trust. If you get to know someone on a social basis, it is more likely that they will do business with you.

This method can outstrip every other promotional method if done correctly. You need the right mix of genuine friendliness and salesmanship. Do not be too pushy, but be pushy enough. You want to build the type of relationship where you can go and visit a person a few days after the function.

Go to networking functions fully prepared. Make sure you know the type of people you want to meet and what you intend to discuss with them. Simply going is not enough; you have to be prepared to work. You need to listen to your prospect closely and really enjoy the conversation. However, you need to be careful not to waste the whole night talking to someone who is never going to do business with you in the first place.

Spend just enough time with each person to build a relationship, and get the appointment you are after. That does not necessarily mean you set an exact time and date – just get their permission to come and see them in the near future. If you do not know whom it is you should be talking to, ask friends to point them out, or better still, ask them to make the introduction.

Sales People & Cold Calling

Hiring more salespeople can be one of the smartest things you will ever do. The most important consideration is whether the sales reps will pay for themselves. Offering a low base salary and a generous commission is the ideal way to ensure this. If they sell a little, you break even. If they sell a lot, you do well.

Generally, you should not have any trouble getting effective salespeople, providing you have a good training system in place. You also need to have sales scripts for them to use. These need to be tested and measured. Remember, if your sales rep is not getting results, chances are it is a bad script. By paying attention to this key area, you can turn almost anybody into an effective sales rep.

Contests

This is generally done in conjunction with another business, although it can be done on your own or through advertising. The best way to start is to ask clients/customers to fill out a ballot. After the contest, be sure to write them a letter or call telling them who won, and that you have a special offer as a consolation prize.

This works well when you have a product or service most people would love to have but do not think they need. Of course, your contest prize could be something other than your product or service, but that will be less effective in attracting the right sort of people.

Seminars & Events

Holding free or paid seminars is a great way to get your prospects in the same room all at once. You need to advertise your seminar in advance, but not too far in advance. Make sure that you are well prepared and rehearse as often as possible before the seminar.

To get some free publicity, approach the local media advertising reps and offer free tickets for them to give to their clients in return for advertising time or space. This will often work, as it is a soft cost for both parties. You need to understand that your seminar is a glorified sales pitch presented in the format of an education session. What this strategy is really designed to do is get you customers. With this understanding, give your prospects enough information and insight into what it is you do to get them interested.

If you have a challenge with writing your seminar scripts, approach a qualified writer to do it for you. Offer a prize for those who attend. This could take the shape of a free consultation, or free product giveaway. Be sure to make the gift worthwhile. The reason you do this is to collect their names and contact details so that you can follow up with them afterwards.

Write A Book

This is an instant way to develop credibility, and it is actually fun too. While it is good for your ego, it also positions you in the marketplace as a leading authority in your field. By becoming a published author, you may soon find customers trying to seek you out.

If you are not capable of writing your own book, approach somebody to do it for you as a ghostwriter. This will cost you some money, but you can lessen your initial outlay by offering them royalties from any books sold. This form of marketing can be extremely effective, allowing you to market yourself as an expert. You may even decide to give the book away free, in order to generate leads. Of course, it does not need to be a long book – a small 10-page booklet could be just enough.

Party Plan

Selling your product via a party plan takes a fair bit of organization but it can be worth the effort. This is where people host a party for their friends and demonstrate your product. Usually, you will supply a demonstrator who will do the selling. The host receives a bonus if a certain amount of product sells.

Generally, party plans are more effective if your target markets are female. You need to make the evening enjoyable with lots of games to keep your guests amused. Also, allow them to try on, touch or use your products if possible, as this will help sell them. If you are selling clothing, make sure that you compliment the people on how they look, and be honest. Investigate a range of different party plan organizations before taking the plunge.

Direct Mail

Write a letter to a mailing list you compile yourself, sourcing the addresses from the Yellow Pages or another directory. If you are attempting to sell solely from the mailing, you will need a much longer and more detailed letter than if you were doing a direct mail campaign with a phone follow-up.

It pays to include a gimmick with the letter, something to help people remember it. The people you will be mailing to will probably receive many letters, so you will need to use an effective headline and powerful offer to get them to respond. Try placing your letter in a hand written envelope so that it gives the impression it is not a business letter.

Trade Longer/Different Hours

If you want to get the jump on your competitors, open at a different time, or for longer hours than they do.

Shopping Centre Promotions

These are generally cost effective, as they get your name advertised directly to people who are already in the centre. You can offer the shopping centre something to give away as a prize in a contest. This will certainly raise your profile.

By setting up a display in a shopping centre, you get the opportunity to demonstrate your goods or services to passing traffic. The trick here is to make it as interesting as possible. You will need to have support materials such as flyers and business cards on hand to give out, but do not rely on these to sell for you – that is your job.

Have someone with a microphone there to explain what you are doing and how it could benefit your audience.

Open Days & Sign-On Days

This technique can work for many different types of businesses. If you advertise it properly, and provide enough incentives (goodies, entertainment, special deals), you are likely to get a good turnout. These days can work as much for their entertainment value as anything else.

Trade Shows

This can work well if you select the right shows in which to participate. Think carefully about the cost, and about how much you need to sell to make that money back. Will you make it back immediately, or in the very short term? Do not go just to "build awareness" – that is exactly the same as "wasting money".

When you plan your display, make sure you do something different – and have something for people to look at. It is also important to get people's names and details, or better yet, arrange to get the list of every person who attends the show from the organizers.

Having demonstrations is a good way to attract people to your booth. You may also wish to pay a professional to promote your display. Running a contest or draw is a great way to get qualified leads, so consider incorporating this into your display. To get people to participate, you need to make the prize worthwhile. Having a "trade show only" special is another way to make good money from this type of event.

Market Days

Markets can work extremely well for certain types of products. It is important to consider that people who come to markets are looking to buy, but only if the price is right. They will buy if they find a real bargain or something completely out of the ordinary.

Location

Sometimes it may be worth considering a change of location altogether, or perhaps opening other locations. When choosing a location, ask yourself the question: "How much new business will I get from being here?", then "Considering that, is the rent reasonable?"

Look for other factors like trees that obscure your signage or bad neighbouring businesses that bring in an unfavourable element.

Before deciding on a location, spend some time there watching the passing traffic, taking note of how many go into the other businesses in that area. You also need to make sure that there is ample, accessible parking. It can be a good idea to talk to other shop owners in the area to get their views on the location. If the majority of them have not been there long, that could be telling you something. Remember, a better location is not the answer to everything, but it sure can help.

Business Cards

People will only hang onto your business cards if you give them a reason to do so in the first place. It pays to put more than just your "name, rank and serial number" on the cards.

Try adding some benefits and profile your uniqueness. While some people like to get creative with the shape and size of their business cards, it is not advisable to do so. The reason is quite simple. Your business card needs to be able to fit into your client's wallet, purse or card holder. If they cannot store it easily, the chances are they will not store it at all.

In order to fit more selling information on your cards, try printing on both sides. This costs more, but not that much more. You might like to print combination business and appointment cards. You would still keep the cards at regulation size, but instead of printing extra text on the back, you would leave space to fill out appointment times instead. It is also a good idea to make sure that your phone number is large and easy to read. Place it in the bottom right corner of your business card, as this is where people will look for it.

Telemarketing

Make sure you are calling a qualified list of people who will be interested in what you are trying to sell. One of the advantages of employing telemarketers is that you can pay them on a commission basis, rather than paying them a wage.

When employing a team of telemarketers, make certain you are getting top people who will sound friendly and relaxed on the phone. You will also need to provide them with a great script that hooks people. Telemarketing can be very effective if you have an incredibly good offer.

Sponsorships

Sponsoring sports teams can work well if you receive a good profile, or obtain naming rights. It is mostly an awareness-building tool, so if you sponsor a local club or team, make sure they allow you to have a list of all members of the club so you can mail to them.

You should also strike up a deal to make sure that their members come to you and not your opposition. Moreover, make sure the club itself only deals through, or with, you. By becoming familiar to the players in the team (or the members of the club), you can build excellent rapport, which will keep them coming back to you for many years to come.

It is also important that your logo appears on their apparel. Make sure it can be clearly seen in any photographs that may appear in the local paper.

Building Signage

In many cases, this will be your most important form of advertising. This especially applies to fast food, restaurants and businesses with high roadside visibility. Make the signage work for you – offer benefits and good deals. Instead of "Computer Upgrades", try something like "Upgrade your old computer for less than $500 here!"

Buy Database Lists

Buy a list of names from a list broker. These lists can be very specific, and you may find what you are looking for. Be careful though – some lists are very poor in quality, so ask questions like how were the names compiled, how old is the list, how many people have mailed to it, how did they go, whether you can talk to them, and are there any guarantees?

Once you have your database, you can then use it for a direct mail or flyer campaign. These lists will generally vary in price, with the more up-to-date and targeted ones obviously costing more.

It is well worth paying extra to get one with a larger number of prospects.

Yellow Pages

This is an excellent advertising vehicle for some products or services, especially the type that people only buy occasionally. The important thing to remember is that your ad must stand out – do something different to what everyone else is doing.

Also remember that your readers are already buyers; they are just deciding whom they should buy from. You can also advertise in more than just your local Yellow Pages.

White Pages

The White Pages are often underrated by businesses. Of course, you cannot advertise here, but it is important that people are able to find you. You may want to consider a bold heading so you are easily seen. Your White Pages listing can also be useful when advertising on a broadcast medium. If you are doing radio, there is no harm in adding the line, "Find us under V in the White Pages" to your script. Also remember the White Pages are available across the country; it could be an idea to list your business in all of them.

Other Directories

Think about how many sales you need to make in order to pay for the listing. If you think it looks reasonable that you will at least recover your investment, then you should place the ad. Keep in mind that if you are going to use another directory, the rules for advertising in the Yellow Pages apply.

In-Store & Sidewalk Signage

As with building signage, this can be your most powerful form of advertising. This applies especially if you are in a shopping centre or shopping strip. Using an 'A-Frame' with a good headline and an arrow can work very well. Don't forget to include an offer.

Catalogues

Mail these out to your existing customers, hand them out in-store, or use them as a mailbox drop. They work particularly well when you have a number of different product categories and many specials.

The front page should offer reasons for your prospect to look inside, so make use of teasers.

Inserts

This is where you arrange for a flyer to be inserted into a newspaper or magazine. These can work well, as they literally fall out at the reader's feet. You will need to have a great headline to ensure people will read your insert.

One thing you can be sure of with this form of advertising - people WILL see your ad. The only thing to look out for, though, is trying to ensure your insert is not part of a group of inserts being distributed in the same edition of the publication. Try to make sure you are the only one running in that publication, if that is possible. The key to success is having a strong offer.

Brochures

These are a great sales aid. Unless your brochure contains compelling headlines, most people will generally only look at the pictures.

If your product is an expensive one, like a car or a house, a brochure could be just the sort of backup you need during the sales process. People will often hang on to a brochure for a long time, so it is worth making it attractive and glossy.

Barter/Trade Exchanges

This method attracts customers to whom you may otherwise not have access. People will come to you just because you are a member of their trade exchange, and they will be less obsessed with price and other buying criteria.

Again, investigate a little first and ask for references. To make the most of this situation, you will need to promote the fact that you are a member in all your other advertisements. Also, make sure that you have an effective ad in their directories, as this could bring you extra business.

Mailbox Flyers

Flyers are a very inexpensive form of advertising that does produce results. Your headline must speak to the reader straight away, and offer something very attractive. Most people resent junk mail, and prefer to respond to flyers that speak to them directly.

Using pictures on your flyers is one way of ensuring they are noticed. You should also consider printing them on unusual paper or cardboard that is cut into different shapes. The main thing to remember when using flyers is that you should not expect to receive a high response.

Flyers can be good for local businesses, such as fast food and home-delivery companies. Trades people can also use flyers to good effect, but as with anything, you need to test and measure on a small scale before you print off thousands.

Sidewalk Handbills

This involves handing out flyers on the street. They can be very effective if you have an incredible offer and your business is just a quick walk from where you are handing out the flyers.

It is important to consider how you will reach your target market, because unless you consider this, most people will simply dump them without giving them a second glance.

The benefit of this type of promotion is that you can choose whom you hand your flyers to – whether they are women, young people or someone more specific. You need to present yourself well and make sure that you are friendly and enthusiastic. If you are doing it in a shopping centre, you will need to check with centre management first as some centres do not allow this type of activity.

Network Marketing

This is the "Amway" style of business. While many would consider networking out of favour, it is still a massive business – networkers spend billions and billions every year. Does your product fit? To find out, ask yourself this question: "Is my product or service so good that anyone who uses it will literally beg their friends to buy it too?"

To understand how it works, and how you can use it in your business, try joining a reputable company like Amway. This gives you a chance to find out the techniques these companies use to not only market their goods, but also how they recruit new members and keep them motivated.

The real benefit to you is that once it is set up, you will no longer need to work at it. You will be able to sit back and enjoy a substantial passive income.

Piggy-Back Invoice Mailings

If you are friendly with another business owner, consider including a flyer or letter with his or her regular invoice mailings.

You could offer to pay for the mail out as an incentive. You could even ask if they will write (or simply sign) a letter recommending your service. In this situation, you need to make it clear that you intend to pay for the cost of printing your flyers or letters. Also, take the time and effort to write an effective marketing piece, even though your letter is certain to make it into the home and be looked at.

Billboards/Posters

These are excellent as a directional medium, where you use the billboard to tell people to take the next left, or that your business is 5 minutes away. It is also a good way to support other promotional media like TV or radio.

Your product or service should have wide appeal, and be simple to understand. It is also a great way to promote a product or service you sell through retailers.

Cash Register Tapes

Advertising on the back of supermarket cash register tapes can work if your ad includes a coupon that people will want to collect. If your business has mass appeal and is local, this can be very effective, especially if your prices appeal to the local "coupon cutters". This option generally works best for lower priced products and services.

Local Weekly Newspaper Advertising

These papers are usually weekly and are sometimes distributed free to the local area. They are becoming more popular as we adopt a far more local or regional focus. Radio, television and the Internet can instantly bring you the world news, but the local newspaper is becoming more focused on events in a certain area. These weekly papers allow even more interaction between the reader and their paper.

This really can be a cost effective way to reach your local market, especially homemakers. The rates are generally affordable as the paper has a shelf life of at least a week. Ninety percent of results come in the first four days, but results will still come in up to six weeks after delivery. The types of businesses that can benefit from this form of advertising are serviced based companies such as plumbers, hairdressers or electricians. One suggestion I have for _____ may be to write a monthly column that highlights

_____ and possibly a product that is directly related to that issue.

Daily Newspaper Advertising

This is your major daily, that is, the paper read by most people. These papers come out daily, and are generally read by people on their way to work, or people interested in keeping up-to-date with world events. They can be expensive, so you need to make sure your product appeals to a wide group of people in order to make it cost-effective.

Usually 90% of your results come within 48 hours. It is best to test and measure which day of the week works best for you. Usually Saturday and Sunday papers out-perform the weekday papers. A good rainy day on Sunday will always boost response. Also, remember to test the section you advertise in.

In these publications, you need to have your advertisement running in the first eleven pages, and on a right hand page. Set your advertisement in the same typeface that the paper itself uses for its articles. By making your advertisement look like an article written by a journalist, you can increase its chance of success. Remember, with this form of marketing you need to have a worthwhile offer and to place a time limit on that offer to make people 'act now'.

Daily papers can work for any type of business, but they are particularly effective when you are having a sale. The sales people from the paper will probably try to convince you to take out a larger advertisement than you really need.

Do not be pushed into it. Only use the minimum amount of space needed to get your message across. Your ad will need to have a powerful headline that grabs your prospect's attention, and do not fall into the trap of trying to use too much white space. Studies have proven that effective use of white space will make your ad more appealing and help communicate your message, but don't overdo it.

Magazine Advertising

This is a great way to go after a very specific target market. It is usually very easy to judge who is reading a magazine by the articles as well as by the other advertisers. People reading magazines will pay attention to the ads, as they generally represent their direct interest. The challenge here is that your competitors will probably be there too.

Because most magazines are national publications, they will generally be very expensive to advertise in. However, the major benefit of advertising in magazines is that they target people with specific interests. For example, a company that manufactures fireplaces would advertise in a House & Home magazine, whereas a hose manufacturer could advertise in a gardening magazine.

Television Advertising

This type of advertising is usually best suited for products and services with mass appeal and high distribution. Because the ad will be seen by people from a diverse geographical area, it needs to be available widely, or accessible by most. Try to add a direct response element, to make it measurable.

Image-building TV ads are not for small business. Make your ads sell. Consider carefully before going into TV, but do not automatically rule it out. Look at it from a financial perspective – how many sales will you generate for your investment?

In some markets, your commercial will be competing with up to four other stations. You need to consider the demographics of each before finalizing your strategy. Television stations will usually be able to make the commercial for you, but because they may not have experienced copywriters available, do not expect them to design effective commercials for you.

You will need to place your commercials in certain time slots. Do not just buy the inexpensive package they offer you, and do not allow them to place the commercials in what is known as 'run of station' time slots. 'Run of station' is where they decide when your commercials will go to air, not you. You need to specify the times that you want the commercials to run.

Trade Journal Advertising

Journals are excellent for reaching a very particular group of professionals or business people. As with magazine advertising, your competitors will also be there, but people will generally take the time to read and evaluate your advertisement.

Trade journals are also one of the least expensive forms of print advertising. Companies advertising in these publications have the advantage of being able to reach a very specific market. Nevertheless, while this is a benefit, it can also be a limitation, as they generally do not have a very high readership. To use trade journals effectively, you need to have a great offer. You can achieve good results from advertising in trade publications, providing a segment of your target market reads them. For example, a life insurance company might advertise in an industrial magazine, as the people who work in that industry are in a higher risk bracket, and may need extra coverage.

Fridge Magnets

Again, a good idea for products or services that are only required rarely. Those supplied by plumbers or electricians are a good example. These can also work for fast food and restaurants.

Joint fridge magnets can also work well. These magnets advertise a range of local businesses and people generally keep them.

Create An Industry Newsletter

Why not publish your own newsletter and send it to every person in the industry? Do not write articles about your business – write them as though the newsletter is a genuinely independent publication. It will eventually be picked up and read by the right people.

Include gossip, pictures and reader letters. By creating your own industry newsletter, you will have full reign to advertise your product whenever you want, and how you want. You can also utilize a mock editorial recommending your business. There may even be the possibility of branching out and selling advertising space to other non-competitive businesses.

One of the best ways to gain higher readership is to talk about new products on the market that you just happen to sell. In this situation, you would write the article as though it were written by someone else. You would then contact the companies that receive the newsletter a few days later to try and sell that product to them.

Radio Advertising

This inexpensive medium is best for products with immediacy. While it is often viewed as good support for TV or print advertising, radio is an effective medium in itself. It is an aggressive medium where you must actively attract listeners through original commercials. Bear in mind that people do not usually listen to the radio actively – it is a background medium – so your ad must really leap out and speak to THEM.

Radio can be very effective for products and services where people take advantage of an advertised offer within the next 24 hours. Radio is also the last advertising medium heard before people go shopping.

Stickers & Tags

Stickers and tags are a great way to advertise a business where the product is bought irregularly yet is unimportant to the buyer. For example, with a printer cartridge supply company, people do not really mind whom they buy from, as long as it is quick, inexpensive and easy. By placing a sticker on the printer, they will always call you when they need a cartridge.

The best way to distribute stickers is to go door-to-door, or to mail them to people with a covering letter.

Car Signage

Network marketers often use this. Nevertheless, do not try to do it yourself – get your signs professionally designed. Do not try to say too much – keep it simple. Think of it as a billboard and use the same sorts of SELLING words as you would on a billboard. Be bold and different with your use of colours and graphics. Moreover, include your phone numbers.

Industry Newsletter Ads

Why not publish your own newsletter and send it to every person in the industry? Do not write articles about your business – write them as though the newsletter is a genuine independent publication. It will eventually be picked up and read by the right people.

Include gossip, pictures and reader letters. By creating your own industry newsletter, you will have full reign to advertise your product or service whenever you want, and how you want – you can also have a mock editorial recommending your business. There may even be the possibility of branching out and selling advertising space to other non-competitive businesses.

One of the best ways to gain higher readership is to talk about new products on the market that you just happen to sell. In this situation, you would write the article as though someone else wrote it. You would then contact the companies that receive the newsletter a few days later to try to sell that product to them.

School Newsletter Ads

Generally, these are very inexpensive, and they offer the advantage of appearing as though you are in part endorsed by the school. This adds credibility and trust. These newsletters are read, and if you offer educational services or products, these publications may bring you some good results. It can also be a good way to reach young mothers. Another advantage to advertising in school newsletters is that most advertisements will not be well written, so you will not have much competition.

Fax Outs

These can work well, as so few businesses use this method. If the fax out is well targeted, or better still, addressed to someone (or at least a position), there is a good chance it will succeed. A phone follow-up makes it more effective still.

You could also consider the mystery fax idea – that is, send a fax addressed to no one. The person who picks it up will take it to everyone and ask, 'Is this yours?' Everyone will get to see it. You should also be careful not to send a fax that is too long – one or two pages are acceptable. Anything longer will make people annoyed, as you will be tying up their fax line. Use a strong headline and only give them enough information to get them interested and call you.

Test & Measure

Just testing and measuring can help increase your number of leads. Knowing where your customers come from gives you the power to make smart decisions about what to spend your marketing money on.

Taxi Backs

This can be an effective way to promote events and make public announcements. Because the only chance people will have to read it is when they are stopped at traffic lights or in heavy traffic, you need to keep your message short and to the point. Try using bright colours and unusual graphics to capture people's attention. You need to emphasize one key point - the one big idea that will get people to respond. Also, make sure that your wording is large and easily read.

Cinema Advertising

There are two types – still and moving. Stills involve displaying a still frame while the announcer reads a script. Moving is where you have a TV commercial playing. Advertisers with a high budget generally only use moving commercials. Still commercials are generally used by smaller businesses with a more modest budget.

Make sure your script speaks directly to the people you want to target. Make them a good offer that encourages them to visit your business. Incidentally, cinema can be a good way to reach people between the ages of 18 and 30.

Blimps, Plane Banners & Skywriting

These are very high profile, and guaranteed to get people looking, and talking. Of course, it is only suitable for large businesses, and generally only works as an awareness builder. It can work very well in the case of a special event, such as "Toyota run-out sale ends in 3 days. Hurry!"

Improve Your Sales Conversions

www.moreprfitlesstime.com | www.ceo-ondemand.com.au

Written Guarantee

This concept is where you write a guarantee that addresses the customer's key frustration in buying from you. For example, a hairdresser could guarantee that you will like your haircut and so will 98% of your friends, or a dentist could guarantee you no pain.

Pick out the one thing that people are scared of when buying from you, and guarantee that it will not be a problem. If it is, offer to refund their money, or put things right. Once you have finalized what it is, make sure you tell people, and advertise it. Almost any business can benefit from using a guarantee. The better the guarantee, the more comfortable people will be when dealing with you. If you are selling high priced items, you may want to look at insurance against ever having to pay out on your guarantee.

Define Your Uniqueness

If there is nothing different about you, people will only buy from you because of convenience, nothing more. Added to that, you will never be able to raise your prices – if there is anyone doing it for less, people will buy from them. You need to work out what is special about you, and publicize it. In addition, do not just say 'price' or 'quality' – these are empty terms. You need to make it very specific and meaningful.

For example, you may promote yourself as the only mechanic who picks up and drops off customers in a limousine. Alternatively, maybe you are an accountant that has a masseur give your clients a massage while you do their tax. There are almost unlimited possibilities when finding your uniqueness. Often just claiming that what you do is unique and then promoting that point is sufficient to have people believe you. This can be the case, even when there are plenty of other people who do exactly the same thing that you do. No matter which business you are in, you need to stress a unique quality, one that people will perceive as being invaluable.

Develop Your Own Product Line/Sell An Exclusive Line

If you have something nobody else has, such as your own product line, people will have to buy it from you. But first you must make that sure your products are up to scratch, and genuinely attractive. There is no point producing a unique product if there is no one in the market place who wants it. Before you start to think of what it is you can produce, stop and ask yourself: "What is it that I can produce that there is a demand for?" This can be a great way for you to get the edge over your competition.

If you market this product effectively, you can place yourself in the position where anyone wanting that product must come to you. Of course, you can then also sell this product to other companies in different markets. For example if you sell the product to your customers in Canada, why not sell the same product wholesale to U.S. companies?

Increase Range Or Variety

The more you have, the more options you can give the customer, and the more individual tastes you can cater to. Naturally, you have to be careful you do not end up buying a bunch of highly specialized stock that you can never sell. In many cases though, going from 'Would you like an apple or an orange?' to 'Would you like an apple, orange or a banana?' can make a big difference. One of the things you need to be mindful of is staying focused on your core business. Increasing your range is fine, but if you try to be all things to all people, you end up being nothing to anyone.

This is particularly true for manufacturing companies. The trap that many of these companies fall into as they start to grow is line extension. The reason this does not work is that people often associate your brand name with your product. When you try to introduce a new and different product to your range under the same brand name, people will not accept it. Not only will they not buy it, but also quite often, the sales of your existing product will suffer, as you will no longer be seen as the specialist in that field.

A good example of this is a company that manufactured dog food. The company decided to try and tap into the condiments market, and released a range of sauces. Unfortunately, they used the same brand name as the one for which their dog food was famous. It is quite obvious why that whole concept was wrong. However, there are many advantages for the small to medium sized business to add extra lines or products. Many businesses fail because they only sell one product, which does not need replacing, or replenishing for extended periods. By offering people an option, or having something else to sell them if they are not interested in your first product, you can greatly increase your number of conversions.

Provide Quality Products

People will buy quality when it is affordable. By providing the best, you put yourself a cut above everyone else. Moreover, do not be afraid to mark up the products – people expect to pay more for quality, and they tend to regard higher priced items as being of a higher standard. While you can offer a range of prices, it would not be appropriate to offer the most expensive product as well as a bargain basement line.

The reason for this is simply that those people looking for quality will view you as being a bargain store, those looking for a bargain, will view you as being too expensive. You need to cater to one group only. You can do this by stocking the highest quality products, and some models that are middle of the range. By providing the very best in quality, you will get a very good reputation in the market place. You will find that quality shoppers are far less likely to hassle you for a better price, and will generally buy on the spot.

Print A Benefits/Testimonials List

You can give this sheet to every person who uses your product or service. It contains the four most important things about your product, or the seven reasons yours is a better choice for them. Make sure you use it each time. Alternately, print testimonials on it (e.g. direct quotes from your past customers about how good you are). A mix of both strategies can work very well. The benefit of using testimonials is that your prospects will find it reassuring that other people have dealt with you and are happy with the results. By doing this, you are almost getting your past customers to do your selling for you. If you do not have any testimonials, ask your past customers to provide you with them. Some may not want to, but you only need a handful that is happy to help and you are well on the way. This can be a great way to close the sale. If your prospect seems interested but is not quite ready to commit, having a list of testimonials from past clients can often tip them over the edge. Of course, a benefit sheet can do the same thing, but you need to make sure that you list only the benefits and not the features of your product.

Demonstrations

If you can demonstrate the product first hand, do it. Because most people are visual, they like to 'see' how things work. This also gives them a chance to experience the product before they buy. If you cannot demonstrate your product, think of a way you can do something similar (e.g. "before & after" photos)? What about samples to give to the person to try? Using taste tests if you are in the food or beverage industry may be another option. Videos are another effective way to demonstrate your product. Because most of the population is visual rather than auditory, showing them how something works is far more effective than trying to explain it to them. If you cannot communicate the benefits to your prospect, how can you expect to sell it? By demonstrating how your product works and what it can do for the consumer, your conversion rate is certain to increase.

Quality Brochures

Having a well-produced full colour glossy brochure can work wonders. It gives you the aura of professionalism, and lets people really take their time to look over your offer in detail. The quality is important if you are selling expensive products. For example if you were trying to sell thousand dollar home stereo systems, you would not want your brochures printed in black and white, and on inexpensive paper. You would want to give the impression of class. If people believe that your business sells quality products, you are far more likely to get qualified prospects coming in to buy. If your brochures make your business look inexpensive and tacky, you are far more likely to attract 'C' and 'D' class clients or customers. The problem with attracting those types of people is that they are far less likely to purchase right away, preferring instead to argue over price. You need to understand that while having a good quality brochure can increase your conversion rate, relying on it to do the selling for you can have an adverse effect. Make sure you still put the effort into selling to the customer yourself.

Offers

To seal the deal, throw in something they did not expect – something that gives them the perception that they are getting a great deal. Then place a time limit on it, which pressures them into making a decision. Make sure it is something that they will value highly which does not cost you very much. You might like to use this as a last resort. If your prospect keeps coming back to price and you cannot get around it, try offering something extra instead. For example, a computer company might offer free software if their client buys a new system from them. Nevertheless, to take advantage of this offer, the client must sign up there and then.

Free advice can be an effective offer. This would give the impression of value, when there is no real hard cost for the company providing it. Take for example our computer store. Instead of offering free software, they may offer to come to your home and set your system up for you. Try to identify a soft cost service that your business can offer.

Packaging

The more attractive the product looks, the better chance there is of selling it. Try re-doing the packaging to make it look more modern or more traditional, depending on what you are trying to achieve. Include the benefits of your product on the side of the package. You may consider including value-added products – smaller accessories that may serve as a lead into another product line. Offering add-on value products can assist you in converting inquiries into sales. Keep this in mind when you are looking over your existing packaging. Also, understand that your product may be competing with others for your prospects attention. Make certain that yours is the one that grabs the customer's attention first.

Display Awards/Certificates

The interesting thing about certificates and awards is that it does not matter what they are, or what they were for, when people see framed awards or certificates, they think: "This place must be good.".

Even team awards will give the impression of quality. The only relevant detail is the year. Displaying something with 1989 prominently showing may damage your chances of making the sale. Awards and certificates give the impression of both quality and credibility. The perception is that if you have won an award, then you are hardly going to be a 'fly by night' type of company.

Because of this extra credibility, you will be able to make extra sales to those people who may otherwise have had some reservations about dealing with you. If you have not won any awards, try starting your own staff awards and then display these. Unless people look closely, they should give the impression that your company has won them. Even if they do see that they are staff and not outside awards, it will still give the impression that your company is credible.

On-Hold Messages

Putting customers on hold can either annoy people, or encourage them to buy. If you must put people on hold, why not take the opportunity to tell them all about your business: why it is so good, what you sell, why they should buy today. Many businesses use basic, annoying, on-hold music. The reason why they do not give more thought to it is quite simple – their own company has never put them on hold. You can also have a local radio station played to clients as they wait, but why waste such an excellent marketing opportunity.

On-hold messages give you the chance to tell your prospects about other products or services they may not know about. If you offer a guarantee, or have a unique selling proposition, this is your chance to let people know about it. This is great for professional people such as lawyers or accountants, or retail stores that get many phone inquiries. In fact, almost any type of business can make use of this sales aid. It is worthwhile getting the tapes professionally done. Nobody wants to listen to somebody who stops, stammers and generally does not have a good voice for this type of recording. While getting a professional to tape your message may cost more, it will be worth it in the end.

Account Applications

When people are buying, offering them an account can often seal the deal. Offer to run through the application procedure on the spot. If they succeed (which they probably will), it is as simple as saying "I will just put that on your account". This will help you make sales simply because people can take the goods now, and pay later. If they do not physically have to take the money out of their wallet or purse, the chances are they will be more than happy to make the purchase. Putting an account system into place is quite straightforward. You can now buy software packages that do it all for you and even tell you when each account is due.

Mail Order

Allowing people to order from home can give you the edge. If you can take the hassle out of the buying procedure, by letting people simply call and order, many customers will not balk at a higher price. More often than not, a buying decision will be made based on convenience, rather than price. By selling via mail order, you can make it hassle-free for customers to deal with you.

One of the things you need to consider if you are looking at selling by mail order is having a great guarantee. Many people are skeptical about buying products through the mail. There have been many frauds in the past, giving this form of marketing a bad name. To overcome this make sure that you have a watertight guarantee that will give the consumer complete peace of mind.

Point Of Sale Displays

What you do inside your shop is just as important as what you do outside – you have to advertise your products just as hard. Work on your displays – make them attractive, and if possible, interactive. Make tester bottles, listening stations, or taste samples always available. If people can experience the product without fear of being pressured, they will, and if they like it, they will buy. You will still need to assist them in their buying decision, but a well-thought out display can certainly help. Instead of going through your entire sales pitch, you can simply explain to them the sizes and colours your product comes in and then close the sale. Place your display in a high traffic area of your store, like the front door, or near a register. People waiting at the register can then look over your display at their leisure. Make sure that they can take anything they want from the display without needing to leave the line-up and lose their place.

Use Payment Plans & Financing

This can get you over one of the biggest and most common hurdles – the price objection. If anyone says, "I cannot afford it", you can say "but there is a way!" Most customers love credit – it allows them to have things they cannot really afford. Payment plans or financing are necessary for anyone selling high priced items. You do not want to miss a sale because the company down around the corner offers payment options and you do not. While the accounting can be a bit of a hassle, the benefits far out-weight the negatives. You may also like to consider adding a small accounting fee on top of the sale price for anybody who wants to take advantage of this option. This would help offset the cost of employing somebody to look after the accounts. In short, if you have ever lost a sale because the customer could not afford your product, you need to look at payment terms.

Take Credit Cards, Cheques & Debit Cards

If someone wants to give you money, take it in whatever form offered. There are set-up costs for merchant accounts, but most businesses find the investment is worth it. There are now agencies that can help you 'check on cheques'. You simply dial a number and find out if there is enough money. The result is no more bounced cheques, and no more reason not to take them. Credit cards can be processed the same way as well as electronically. You will have to pay an ongoing fee on your debit card set-up, but for the sake of making extra sales, this is well worth it. Almost any business can offer debit card payment, from a supermarket to a pet store. Portable units are also available so mobile companies like windshield repairers or mobile hairdressers can also offer this facility. While not everybody carries cash on them nowadays, very few people would not have a chequebook, credit card or debit card. Not offering these services means that people have to go out of their way to get their money before they can come and do business with you. The reality is that they will soon stop going out of their way, and will start to go to someone else.

Audio & Video Sales Demonstrations

Why do all the hard work yourself – put your best sales story on to tape (audio or video) then let it run continuously. People will stop and look, or tune in and listen. You can also send these tapes in the mail before an appointment, or follow up on the phone and sell directly. This is much less expensive than salesperson!

The quality of production is very important here. Use an outside 'talent' if your own voice is not suitable – you should be able to find someone at your local radio or television station. Hiring someone to make your video is also worthwhile. While some professional companies will charge you a small fortune to produce such a video, you can normally find smaller 'wedding video' type companies that can do it for much less. Unless you are trying to make your product look inexpensive you should stay away from the home video option.

Reprint Press Articles

If you have had anything printed about you (well, anything positive anyway), photocopy it and send it to potential customers. This shows that other people know about you, and that you have a degree of 'celebrity'.

Press articles add a degree of credibility to you and your store, as people view anything written by a journalist as being fact. They see that someone else has said something good about you, rather than you just promoting yourself. To take full advantage of this, get them blown up and place them around your operation in key locations.

Re-Write Quotes, Tenders & Proposals Into Action Plans

Instead of just writing a standard quote (you get X for $Y – take it or leave it), why not write the prospect a letter. Include the price near the top and explain everything that makes you different below it. There is more to their decision than price, so make your letter a Plan of Action, and reflect that. End with "I will call in the next few days to discuss further."

This is important if your product or service is more expensive than your competitors. Explain to your prospect, how much better off they will be if they chose you. Even if you are less expensive than your opposition, do not rely on price alone to win you the job. Some people may view the least expensive as not being good enough. Use your quotes, tenders and proposals to sell to your clients and you will dramatically increase your conversion rate.

Print Your Company's Vision Statement

Write out why you are in business and your own personal standards. Include a summary of your values and company's ethics that outline how you deal with customers. Then give it to every prospect – it will impress them. Or you could get a local print shop to design and print it on nice paper. Have your vision statement professionally mounted and then hang it in clear view of your customers. This way you will have the chance to demonstrate your high level of expertise. If people believe that you are professional, they will be more inclined to do business with you.

Use Prospect Questionnaires

Instead of going through the normal sales process, why not give the prospect a questionnaire. Make it short, and wait with them while they fill it out. Then, make your proposal fit their needs exactly. If they do not want to spend what you quote, suggest that you could do it for the price they want, but they may need to sacrifice a few things.

This gives you the advantage of being able to justify your prices, and the reason that you have recommended product 'X'. It is pretty hard for your prospect to say that what you are offering does not fit with what they had in mind, if you have their questionnaire in your hand. To work out whether you could benefit from using questionnaires, think of all the objections that people normally throw at you during your sales pitch. Then write down questions that would cover those objections by identifying what your prospect is really looking for.

High Dress Standards/Uniforms

People base much of their decision making on your appearance. If you look untidy, customers may perceive lower standards are being met. If you look professional, they will prefer to deal with you. Uniforms are ideal, as they add credibility and the feeling that the customer is dealing with a well-established, big organization. Nametags also work well, and allow the customer to feel they know you. Uniforms are particularly important for any businesses that sell door to door, or those who provide services in peoples' homes.

If you look shabby when the prospect opens the door, it is very unlikely that they will want to do business with you. Choose colours that are subtle and practical. There's no point having white overalls if you are crawling around in peoples' basements. You also need to find suitable material for your uniforms. A mechanic would need a thick, hard wearing type of fabric, while a receptionist may need a lighter material if the office they are working in is warm.

Try Before You Buy

If you can use this strategy safely, then do it. It is the old 'puppy dog' technique – try taking a puppy home and then return it two weeks later. Obviously, people will not have that kind of attachment to the product (unless you sell pets), but the product will become part of their life. It will be twice as easy to say, "On which credit card would you like to pay for that?" This can also take a lot of the risk out of the purchase for the consumer. By being able to test it first, your client can make sure that your product fits their needs. If you do not want to unpack a new product, ask your supplier to provide you with a demo model. This avoids the hassle of goods being returned in a condition, which would make it hard to resell. If you truly believe in the product you are selling, then you would be well advised to let your customers try it out first. Most people will be too lazy to bring your goods back even if they do not find them that appealing.

Sales Scripts

Sales scripts are absolutely essential for each and every business. Once you find the right (or very close to right) way to sell something to someone, why change it? Write down exactly what you said and do it the same way every time. And make sure your team does the same.

Every customer is different, but the objective is always the same – match the product to the buyer. You should have scripts for everything – from answering the phone to saying goodbye. Scripts are very important for your conversion rate. If you change what you say to each customer, how can you expect to be consistent? It is vitally important that you Test and Measure a variety of scripts to find the most effective one for you and your product.

Build Trust & Rapport

There are some simple things you can do to make sure this happens. First, always use your clients' name, and make sure you introduce yourself using your full name. Ask them questions, and genuinely listen to the response – these are your clues. Provide ideas and advice, and do your best to help them. If you believe in your product or service, you should know that one of the best ways to help them is to sell them something.

Be honest with your clients, as dishonesty will destroy any chance of a long term working relationship. It is important that your entire team takes this approach to your customers. There can be few things more disappointing to a salesperson than to take the time and effort to build a relationship, only to have somebody else ruin it. A prime example of this would be the situation where a client has forgotten to make a payment on their account. If the company accountant noticed this and then called them demanding immediate payment or else, the relationship could be destroyed forever.

Educate On Value, Not Price

Remember that people want a good deal, not the least expensive. They will be happier spending the dollars to get something that does exactly what they want, rather than spending less on a product that only does half the job. Explain why some people charge less, and what the prospect will miss if they do it on the cheap. A good way to go about this is to write all the benefits down so you have them clear in your mind.

You might even consider printing these on a fact sheet, which you can then hand to your prospects. Do not simply write: "This is why we are better than they are ..." –You can be a little more subtle but still make sure that your clients know they cannot get the same quality and service from your competition. Things such as after sale service and extended warranties are a good starting point when you are listing your benefits. You need to identify the areas that the customer may have concerns about and then demonstrate how, by dealing with you, they will not have those problems.

Increase Product Knowledge

It is important to know as much about your product or service as you can – the more confident you sound when talking about it, the more likely your prospects are to regard you as the expert. People like to buy from people who appear to know what they are talking about; it gives them a sense of security.

By learning more about what your product does or service accomplishes, what their limitations are and the benefits of them versus the competition, you will be in a better position to sell it. People will always ask questions before they decide to buy. The more expensive the item, the more questions they will ask. By knowing your product inside and out, you will be able to answer these in a confident manner.

Up-Sell, Cross-Sell & Down-Sell

If you are having trouble selling something to a prospect, why not shift the focus to a different product. If it is lack of quality, sell them a higher priced item. If it is too high a price, show them something you have that is less expensive. Alternately, shift the focus to a model of a different color, size or different shape. It is hard enough getting customers in your door, without letting them get away because the model you are trying to sell is not quite what they are after. With this in mind, it is

50   www.moreprfitlesstime.com | www.ceo-ondemand.com.au

important that you do not run one product down in order to sell another. By doing this, it makes it impossible to sell them the one you have been running down, even if it is more in line with what they are really after. To avoid this situation, ask them a lot of questions right up front so that you can gauge what they want, and how much they are willing to spend.

Use NLP Techniques

There are so many little tricks you can use to build rapport with people. For example, by 'matching and mirroring' (that is, copying the body language of your prospect) you will build instant rapport. You will instantly seem more trustworthy and familiar. This alone can win you the sale. Understanding individual personality traits is one area, which can greatly increase your conversion rate. Take for example somebody who is a task oriented and outgoing person. If you were dealing with someone with that particular personality trait, you would be best off sticking to the facts, rather than trying to be their friend. On the other hand, someone who is reserved but more people oriented, would probably prefer you to show an interest in their particular needs. This type of person would not respond well to hard sell techniques. There are many books on these subjects, which will teach you how to identify personality traits of individuals, and then how to effectively communicate with them.

Sell On Emotion & Dreams

People tend to make their decisions based on emotion, not logic. In fact, on average, emotion represents 88% of the decision. Do not be afraid to get emotional with them – not in a teary-eyed way, but just by tapping into what makes them want the item. What are they going to use it for? How are they going to feel when they hold it in their hands? What will their partner think? Ask a few probing questions and then when you get their response, dig a little deeper to find out what they really want.

The person, who says they want a lawn mower to cut grass, could mean that they are not happy with the way their house looks. On the other hand, maybe their partner is giving them a hard time about it. In this situation, rather than focusing on how many horsepower the engine is, try to talk to them about what they will do with the rest of their weekend when this new mower flies through the job. Many people will not be conscious of their true motive for making a purchase. By asking the right questions and then listening closely to their response, you can find out what is really motivating them. Once you have found out, emphasize how they can achieve that goal by using your product or service.

Follow Up & Follow Up Again

Do not let anyone slip through your fingers. Until then, they are still a 'hot' prospect. Try different techniques for getting in touch with them again. You might try explaining to them that you forgot to mention the extra warranty that is available, or the payment plans that your store offers. As a last resort, you could try calling them to offer them a lower price. If you take this approach, make sure that you explain that it is a new, once off promotion and that it is not going to last long. More often than not, your persistence will pay off. However, you need to qualify your prospect before going all out to make the sale. If they do not have the money, or were not interested in your goods in the first place, you can waste a lot of time chasing your tail. Only go after the people that are red-hot prospects.

Ask For The Sale

Do not be shy. If you have asked enough questions, you should have established that the person wants to buy what you sell. If that is the case, assume the sale – ask them an assumptive question, "would you like to pay for that on credit card, or by cash?" A common mistake among many sales people is their need to talk too much, and justify the price. If they are very interested in your product, you probably will not have to do too much at all. In this situation, you simply need to answer a few questions and then close the sale. If you try to explain things in too much detail, the customer could go cold thinking that you are trying to hide something. The trick is to ask temperature-checking questions such as – "How does that fit with what you have in mind?" If the response to this question is positive then close the sale. If the prospect has some reservations, ask them what you would have to do to make it fit in with their plans. By asking these simple questions, you can make a huge difference to your conversion rate.

1-800 Number & Reply Paid Address

Make it simple for people to deal with you. A toll-free number and reply paid address means the barriers to people buying are slightly lower. If your competitors are offering this kind of service, you must also.

Run Contests

Run a contest where the prize is something that will be super-attractive to your target market. You can arrange the prize at an excellent price, or perhaps even free, as the company supplying it will be getting advertising as a result. Of course, you can offer the prize yourself – for example, entrants could win the purchase free. The only way they can enter is if they buy TODAY. Another way to increase your conversion rate through a contest is to offer free entry to anybody who makes a minimum dollar purchase. If the prize is of a high-perceived value to the customer, it can assist you in getting them to sign on the dotted line.

Accept Trade-Ins

This gives you the edge – it means that people can kill two birds with one stone. They can buy something new, and get rid of the old. It also means you can charge a premium price.

You can sell the old model to other customers, or sell it to another business. Alternately, if possible, you may want to break it down for parts.

There are two key ways that trade-ins can help you close the sale. If the prospect is interested in your product, but has bought something similar not long ago, it is unlikely they will want to buy another. The reason, of course, is that they feel they have not yet gotten value for money from the one they already own. Nevertheless, if they can trade-in their existing product on your brand new one, then they will probably feel that they have gotten a good deal.

Scarcity & Limits

Use the best motivators in the world – fear and pain. If people think they are going to miss out, there is a good chance it will swing the sale your way. That is especially so if you also infer that you cannot get any more stock when it sells out. Many people understand this sales tactic, so you need to be subtle and truthful.

Give Away To Get Back

If you start the relationship unselfishly, offering advice and assistance, you will discover that you will ultimately be rewarded with a sale. Although this may not immediately improve your conversion rates, it will over a period of time.

If you are going to be giving away your time, you need to be careful that you do not end up doing too much for no return. You also need to be careful not to fall into the trap of giving people so much information that they believe they can do it themselves. In many cases, being helpful beyond the call of duty can bring you great results. The true advantage of this is not the sale you make to the person you help; it is the people they tell who will then also come to you.

Charge For Normally Free Advice

This will set you up as the expert and put you in a far better position when it comes to the final decision. The prospect will feel in some way obligated to buy from you – after all, they paid you to tell them to. Most people will feel more comfortable buying from a professional. The perception is that if they have to pay to talk to you, then you must know your subject.

Because the people you are talking to will be hanging on your every word, you will be in a better position to tell them to buy now rather than later.

A Gift Cheque Towards Purchase

Include a gift certificate with your letter, which people can spend on anything you have to offer. This works best when your product is mid-priced, and the voucher accounts for about 10-15% of the total price.

To make this strategy even more effective, place a time limit on when the cheque can be used by. This gives your promotion a sense of urgency. The beauty of this sort of promotion is that customers, who may not have bought a product that costs $119, will probably buy it if you have already given them $20 towards it. Giving your customers a gift certificate also means they have to buy from you rather than your opposition.

Allow Pre-Payment

Allow people to pay before the goods have arrived. You may even want to offer a discount, or an added value product to encourage this. By letting people pay for items in advance you can make it easier for them to pay the product off. Because some people do not like putting things on credit, you can entice them to buy from you by offering this service. A pre-payment discount can also be just the thing to help you close the sale. It does not need to be a huge saving, but it must be enough to make it worth their while. Because your customers will actually be paying for something they have not yet received, you may need to back this up with a good guarantee.

Target Better Prospects

Look at the way you attract prospects. Are you getting the right sort of people? If not, how else could you advertise? It is important to remember that some prospects are more trouble than they are worth.

Change Your Direct Mail Pieces

You should be constantly improving your marketing material. Once it works, keep using it, but occasionally try something different. Trends change as do people's values and the things that appeal to them. If you have been using a direct mail piece for some time, and you have noticed that the response has dropped off quite a bit, it may be time to change it. Be sure to test and measure new pieces to find out what works and what does not work. You may find something as simple as changing the headline on your existing letter is all that is needed.

Your offer is also something that could bring improved results. All types of businesses can use direct mail to promote their goods and services. There are many different factors that can affect the success of your campaign, such as the time of year or the quality of the list you are mailing to. Keep this in mind when you begin to Test and Measure.

Develop Your Own Product Line / Sell An Exclusive Line

If you have something nobody else has, such as your own product line, people will have to buy it from you. Of course, you must make sure your products are up to scratch, and genuinely attractive.

Entertain, Wine & Dine

This is the classic way to encourage people to buy – build a strong relationship with them. This is especially the case if it is an expensive service. People buy as much on your personality as on the merits of your product or service. A little entertaining can go a long, long way, especially when your product or service is also top notch.

Measure Conversion Rates

When you do measure, you will find almost invariably that your conversion rate improves.

Train Your Team In Sales

Your business will only be as good as your employees are and most importantly, as your frontline salespeople. Get them to watch videos, read books and attend seminars. Do not be afraid to pay for all of this – it is an investment in your business. If you do not have the ability to train your team yourself, consider paying someone to come and do it for you.

Your team needs to be able to handle any objections that customers throw up. By using sales scripts and other techniques such as positive body language, they will be able to consistently improve their results. If you are employing new salespeople, you need to have a training program in place when they start. This should be a standardized system that everyone follows.

Ideally, your new team members should read your mission statement, and familiarize themselves with your products and procedures before they get to deal with any clients. Have a more senior sales person orient them initially and then monitor their progress from that point on.

Provide Team Incentives

If you offer something truly valuable, your sales team will try harder. It does not even need to be a prize – it could just be that they get to go home three hours early. Alternatively, you could offer a dinner gift certificate for the month's highest selling sales person. Make the incentive challenging to win, yet accessible to all salespeople. If you have one 'top gun' who always wins, the others will gradually become disenchanted and may stop trying. You could have one for the best service, one for the best ethics, and so on. You might also consider basing the award on a percentage increase that each person achieves month over month. For example, consider the scenario where your leading sales rep sells $45,000 worth of product one month and then $49,500 the next. That would be an increase of 10%. If in this situation another sales rep sold $10,000 one month and then $11,500 the next, they would win. This is because although their total sales were $38,000 less than the other sales person, their percentage increase over the previous month is 5% higher than the leading rep.

Bulk Buy Specials

Encourage people to buy in bulk from you, and offer a significant saving if they do so. This also 'ties' the person up for some time – you have loaded them up with stock, so they will not go anywhere else for quite a while. They will also get used to using your product or service. Bulk specials can encourage the prospect to purchase from you on the spot because of the excellent value for money they will receive.

Collect All Prospect Details

This is essential. Ask every person you deal with if they would like to join your mailing list. Most will say yes and give you whatever details you ask for. From then on, you can follow-up.

Company Profile

This can work as a serious sales tool – create a 5-6 page document detailing what makes your company so great. More importantly, talk about why your company is the best choice for the prospect – and what you plan to do for them! A company profile can give the consumer confidence in you.

Gimmick With Direct Mail

Include something out of the ordinary with your letter. This will ensure your direct mail letter is remembered when you phone. Use your imagination when trying to think of suitable items to use. For example, you might consider including a tea bag or a small toy with your letter. The possibilities are endless. To help you get an idea of the types of gimmicks you can include, try looking in a shop that specializes in inexpensive items. Anything from a coffee mug to a Band-Aid could work in making your letter standout. You need to understand that simply sending a letter is not enough; it needs to grab your prospect's attention. By including something unusual, you can greatly improve the chances of your letter being read.

Offer Exclusivity

Letting people know that they have the opportunity to be your only client can make them feel excited. It can also have the impact of making them want to buy now so they do not miss the deal. The reason this works so well is that it offers your customers a chance to feel special. Inviting them to an 'invitation only' sale can really get them inspired to buy.

Set Sales Targets

Give your salespeople a clear idea of what you need them to achieve. Explain the exact reasons why they need to achieve it, and outline your financial situation. Offer bonuses if they meet their targets. By doing this you will be giving them the extra incentive they need to convert more sales.

Their effort and enthusiasm will improve the closer they get to their target, with the result being better customer service.

Increase Your Clients Spending

Increase Your Prices

The most obvious way to increase your average dollar sale is to increase your prices.

Up Sell

Encourage people to buy a better version of what they are intending to buy. It is especially good for anything which is modular – that is, you can have x and y, or x, y and z included.

Cross Or Add On Sell

Encourage the customer to buy something else that they were not planning on. A technique that is successfully used by companies like McDonalds – "Would you like fries with that?" It can be very effective when selling products that are used in conjunction with others.

Down Sell

Sell the customer something that has a lower price. It sure beats losing the sale.

It can be extremely effective when dealing with customers who cannot afford your expensive items.

Use A Checklist

Simply run through a checklist with your client whenever they purchase a particular type of product.

Use A Questionnaire

If you are unsure of any additional products or services that you could sell, a simple questionnaire can be effective.

Allow Payment Terms / Finance

Allow your customers to spend more by giving them the chance to pay it off over a period of time.

Carry Exclusive Lines

Sell products or services that people cannot get elsewhere. It is an essential technique when you sell products that are common and very price competitive such as computers or cars.

Rearrange Store Layout / Merchandising

Lay out your store so that every product you sell can be seen.

Point Of Sale Material

These take the form of shelf talkers, bin labels, and are available from your suppliers. Again, they are excellent for businesses that have a large range of goods, as well as for businesses that sell accessories to support the main purchase.

Impulse Buys

Place impulse items like chocolates or magazines at cash registers to tempt people as they wait. The longer they wait, the greater the chance of them weakening. Impulse buys can also be placed throughout the store. For example, flashlights next to batteries, mops with buckets, and paintbrushes with paint.

Sell With An Either/Or Question

Just as you are about to finalize a deal with your client consider asking if they would like to purchase either the expensive model or some additional products that complement their purchase. This is especially good when there is a way to up-sell or add-on sell, but you find it challenging to do so.

Create Package Deals

An excellent way to move more items is to offer a discounted rate to customers who buy them as part of a package deal.

Create Bulk Buy Deals

Give people a discount if they buy a certain number, or an extra-large size.

Allow Debit Cards, Cheques & Credit Cards

This is one of the most important systems you can offer. This can increase your average dollar sale by allowing customers to spend more than they have in their wallet. Credit cards in particular are helpful if you are trying to up or add on sell. If they can have the better model and do not have to pay for it right away, they will take it more often than not.

Make Sure Clients Know Your Full Product & Service List

Place signs around your business to inform your customers of the other things you do or stock. It is also important that your sales team educate the customer on these products/services as they serve them. Most business owners mistakenly assume their customers know about everything they sell. The fact is they are usually aware of less than one quarter of everything you sell.

Gift With $XX Purchase

Offer your clients a gift if they exceed a minimum expenditure.

Charge Consulting Fees

Offer to consult with people in your area of expertise.

Sell Service Contracts

People will pay you a little extra to have you service the equipment you have sold them.

When selling a product that needs regular maintenance, you should make use of service contracts. This means that the customer will have all the servicing done by you. A good example is an engineer who sells machinery to a large factory – it is essential to try to sell a service contract.

There may be more profit in the service than in the actual machine. Arrange the service contract at the time of purchase for best results and offer it at a good price. You need to emphasize how important having regular service is.

Sell Extra Warranty/Insurance

Offer to cover the item for longer for an extra charge.

Train Your Team

Help your team in developing skills so they can sell more and do better with up-sells and add-on sales.

Use Sales Scripts

A sales script is an actual "script", outlining the exact words to say when dealing with a customer.

Every business from the smallest to the largest – can benefit from using a sales script. For example, a bed store could write down the entire sales process, from the greeting, to the questions you ask every customer, right up to the final words you use to close the sale. Sales scripts work extremely well when used correctly. Every sales person must use them, every time. An example would be to say: "Hi, have you been in here before?" instead of: "Hi, can I help you." Scripts should include add on products that the customer may need to go with their original purchase.

Train Your Customers

Training your customers is all about doing things in a particular way, so next time they know what to expect.

Create A Quality Image

Present your store and your team members as being professional and upscale. If it fits in with the vision for your business, this can certainly help. This is excellent when quality is important to the customer, and there is no one in the market providing real professionalism.

Only Service "A" Grade Customers

Categorize your customers and eliminate the ones that are annoying, price-driven, and unreliable.

This must be exercised with some caution – you need to be in demand and have many customers. If your business has unique products and is "A" class itself, you can afford this luxury.

Allow Trade-Ins/Trade-Ups

By allowing trade-ins, you solve your customer's problem of what to do with the old product.

Offer Home Delivery

Another way to make it easy for people to deal with you is by offering home delivery.

Charge For Delivery/Mail & Packaging

Simply offer to package and mail items for customers at a fee.

Build Rapport/Treat As Special

By using simple techniques like always calling your clients by their first name, you will build rapport and trust. Of course, the more they trust you, the more you can convince them to buy.

Set An Average Dollar Sale Goal

Set average dollar sale goals for each member of your team. This is especially important when you have sales people working for you. It is also important when your staff are essentially order takers.

Customer Incentives For Bigger Purchases

Give a special bonus if customers spend more than a certain amount.

Measure The Average $$ Sale

This is as simple as it sounds, and works precisely because you are focusing on this area of your business. This is important for every business, especially those with a real opportunity to increase your average dollar sale.

Measuring will point out to your team exactly how well (or poorly) they are performing in this area. Place your average $$$ sale chart on the wall and adjust it daily. If your team knows you are measuring it, they will no doubt try to improve it.

This is especially good if you are having trouble increasing your average dollar sale, yet have a decent amount of margin to play with. For example, you could offer points or funny money that is given out for each dollar spent. When your client reaches a certain number of points, they can receive a discount off their next purchase. Funny money can be honoured as real money that is then used for future purchases. A good idea is to offer $1 funny money for each $10 spent. The idea is to get your customers to spend more than they normally would just to earn extra points.

Team Incentives For Bigger Sales

Offer your team bonuses if they perform better than average. Naturally, there needs to be an opportunity to perform better – if your team is simply selling one product and they sell it to pretty much everyone who comes in, they are limited.

You could set targets for your team and offer a bonus of some kind for each one achieved. List the different prizes available beside each goal. Running it over the course of a month will keep the enthusiasm high amongst the team members.

Stop Discounting

That means exactly what it says – DO NOT discount for any reason.

This will work in most industries, but only if you have a genuine reason why people should pay more to deal with you. This reason needs to be something that appeals to the customer. Simply do not discount your prices. This will mean that your sales are returning the highest possible profit margins. If your customers shop around a lot, you may wish to offer some additional incentives such as free home delivery to assist you in closing the sale. It is important that you educate your customers on the value of doing business with your store.

The one caveat is clear – if you are not any better, you cannot charge more.

Add Value

Offer added value services to encourage customers to buy from you. This could be something like a free first service with each used car sold, or half price scotch guarding on furniture. Try offering these on the deluxe models only to entice your customers to spend more.

Give Away Perceived Value

Give away products or services to make it look like your customers are getting excellent value for money. This will work if you have items that cost you next to nothing, yet have a high-perceived value. In other words, the customer views it as something that they would pay a high price for (relatively speaking).

In Store Promotions

Run special promotions on a regular basis to create interest in your store.

Red Light Specials

Every time you flash a red light (like a police light), people may take advantage of a special.

Educate On Value, Not Price

This is all about concentrating on the product and the benefits, not how much you are selling it for.

You need to get your client focused on the benefits of the product and not the price. This is very important when dealing with bargain hunters or when selling higher priced and luxury items. Remember, if you were no different and no better, why would a customer pay any more to deal with you?

Ask People To Buy Some More

It is all about "ask and you shall receive". If you are not doing it, you should be – people do not mind being asked, just as long as you know when to accept "no" for an answer. You will get the best results with this technique if the items you are selling are about to increase in price, or go out of stock.

4 For The Price Of 3 Offers

Allow people to take four and only charge them for three. This is a great way to encourage people to buy more than they really need. Once again, the best results come from semi-disposable items. Almost any business can use this type of promotion. Try getting your suppliers to assist with the cost of the promotion by giving you some free stock.

Buy One Get One Free Offers

These promotions can be used to great effect where there is a reasonable mark-up on most goods, or when you want to clear old stock. It outsells two for the price of one, or half price and 50% off, by more than double.

In Store Video Promotions

Play videos to demonstrate the features and benefits of a product that you have on sale.

Store, Team & Vehicle Appearance

This is all about paying attention to the visual presentation of your business. A professional appearance is one of the most important considerations in marketing your business, whatever it is. For example, nice clothes and a standard uniform give your customers the impression that you are a quality organization that has pride in its service. All staff should be dressed in the same clothes featuring your corporate logo.

Suggest Most Expensive First

Try to sell the customer the most expensive thing you have first. They may be convinced to buy the more expensive item if you immediately communicate its benefits. You should never assume that your customers want inexpensive products. If they cannot afford the more expensive product, you then have the option to sell the lower priced item.

Provide A Shopping List

This is an extension of the checklist strategy where you actually provide the customer with a list of items they may need to complete a particular project.

Have A Minimum $$ Order Amount

Have a rule that prevents people buying unless they spend a certain amount. Many pizza and takeout food stores will not deliver to your home unless you spend a minimum amount of money. This strategy is also a good idea for plumbers or mechanics with a 24-hour service. Some companies also charge a minimum purchase price for people wishing to withdraw money on debit cards, or who use a credit card.

Allow Lay-Away

Lay-away is where people are able to claim the item and pay off a little bit each week until they own it. Although lay-away is outdated in the age of credit cards and interest free finance, it has the added advantage of bringing them into your store on a regular basis to make payments.

Obviously, this gives you the chance to show them any new products that you can attempt to sell them.

Your Business Action Plan

Action Plan – Mastery Level

Priority	Task	Individual Responsible	Investment	Start Date	Complete Date
	Lead Generation				
High-Moderate-Low	Referral System				
High-Moderate-Low	Press Releases				
High-Moderate-Low	Post Card Mailings				
High-Moderate-Low	Named Promotional Gifts				
High-Moderate-Low	Window Displays				
High-Moderate-Low	Host Beneficiary				
High-Moderate-Low	Internet/Web Pages				
High-Moderate-Low	Strategic Alliances				
High-Moderate-Low	Networking Functions				
High-Moderate-Low	Sales People & Cold Calling				
High-Moderate-Low	Contests				
High-Moderate-Low	Seminars & Events				
High-Moderate-Low	Write A Book				
High-Moderate-Low	Party Plan				
High-Moderate-Low	Direct Mail				
High-Moderate-Low	Trade Longer/Different Hours				
High-Moderate-Low	Shopping Centre Promotions				
High-Moderate-Low	Open Days & Sign-On Days				
High-Moderate-Low	Trade Shows				
High-Moderate-Low	Market Days				

Priority	Task	Individual Responsible	Investment	Start Date	Complete Date
High-Moderate-Low	Location				
High-Moderate-Low	Business Cards				
High-Moderate-Low	Telemarketing				
High-Moderate-Low	Sponsorships				
High-Moderate-Low	Building Signage				
High-Moderate-Low	Buy Database Lists				
High-Moderate-Low	Yellow Pages				
High-Moderate-Low	White Pages				
High-Moderate-Low	Other Directories				
High-Moderate-Low	In-Store & Sidewalk Signage				
High-Moderate-Low	Catalogues				
High-Moderate-Low	Inserts				
High-Moderate-Low	Brochures				
High-Moderate-Low	Barter/Trade Exchanges				
High-Moderate-Low	Mailbox Flyers				
High-Moderate-Low	Sidewalk Handbills				
High-Moderate-Low	Network Marketing				
High-Moderate-Low	Piggy-Back Invoice Mailings				
High-Moderate-Low	Billboards/Posters				
High-Moderate-Low	Cash Register Tapes				
High-Moderate-Low	Local Weekly Newspaper Advertising				

JOHN MILLAR

Priority	Task	Individual Responsible	Investment	Start Date	Complete Date
High-Moderate-Low	Daily Newspaper Advertising				
High-Moderate-Low	Magazine Advertising				
High-Moderate-Low	Television Advertising				
High-Moderate-Low	Trade Journal Advertising				
High-Moderate-Low	Fridge Magnets				
High-Moderate-Low	Create An Industry Newsletter				
High-Moderate-Low	Radio Advertising				
High-Moderate-Low	Stickers & Tags				
High-Moderate-Low	Car Signage				
High-Moderate-Low	Industry Newsletter Ads				
High-Moderate-Low	School Newsletter Ads				
High-Moderate-Low	Fax Outs				
High-Moderate-Low	Test & Measure				
High-Moderate-Low	Taxi Backs				
High-Moderate-Low	Cinema Advertising				
High-Moderate-Low	Blimps, Plane Banners & Skywriting				
	Conversion Rate				
High-Moderate-Low	Written Guarantee				
High-Moderate-Low	Define Your Uniqueness				
High-Moderate-Low	Develop Your Own Product Line/Sell An Exclusive Line				
High-Moderate-Low	Increase Range Or Variety				

Priority	Task	Individual Responsible	Investment	Start Date	Complete Date
High-Moderate-Low	Provide Quality Products				
High-Moderate-Low	Print A Benefits/Testimonials List				
High-Moderate-Low	Demonstrations				
High-Moderate-Low	Quality Brochures				
High-Moderate-Low	Offers				
High-Moderate-Low	Packaging				
High-Moderate-Low	Display Awards/Certificates				
High-Moderate-Low	On-Hold Messages				
High-Moderate-Low	Account Applications				
High-Moderate-Low	Mail Order				
High-Moderate-Low	Point Of Sale Displays				
High-Moderate-Low	Use Payment Plans & Financing				
High-Moderate-Low	Take Credit Cards, Cheques & Debit Cards				
High-Moderate-Low	Audio & Video Sales Demonstrations				
High-Moderate-Low	Reprint Press Articles				
High-Moderate-Low	Re-Write Quotes, Tenders & Proposals Into Action Plans				
High-Moderate-Low	Print Your Company's Vision Statement				
High-Moderate-Low	Use Prospect Questionnaires				
High-Moderate-Low	High Dress Standards/Uniforms				
High-Moderate-Low	Try Before You Buy				
High-Moderate-Low	Sales Scripts				

JOHN MILLAR

Priority	Task	Individual Responsible	Investment	Start Date	Complete Date
High-Moderate-Low	Use Prospect Questionnaires				
High-Moderate-Low	High Dress Standards/Uniforms				
High-Moderate-Low	Try Before You Buy				
High-Moderate-Low	Sales Scripts				
High-Moderate-Low	Build Trust & Rapport				
High-Moderate-Low	Educate On Value, Not Price				
High-Moderate-Low	Increase Product Knowledge				
High-Moderate-Low	Up-Sell, Cross-Sell & Down-Sell				
High-Moderate-Low	Use NLP Techniques				
High-Moderate-Low	Sell On Emotion & Dreams				
High-Moderate-Low	Follow Up & Follow Up Again				
High-Moderate-Low	Ask For The Sale				
High-Moderate-Low	1-800 Number & Reply Paid Address				
High-Moderate-Low	Run Contests				
High-Moderate-Low	Accept Trade-Ins				
High-Moderate-Low	Scarcity & Limits				
High-Moderate-Low	Give Away To Get Back				
High-Moderate-Low	Charge For Normally Free Advice				
High-Moderate-Low	A Gift Cheque Towards Purchase				
High-Moderate-Low	Allow Pre-Payment				
High-Moderate-Low	Target Better Prospects				
High-Moderate-Low	Change Your Direct Mail Pieces				
High-Moderate-Low	Develop Your Own Product Line / Sell An Exclusive Line				

www.moreprfitlesstime.com | www.ceo-ondemand.com.au

Priority	Task	Individual Responsible	Investment	Start Date	Complete Date
High-Moderate-Low	Train Your Team In Sales				
High-Moderate-Low	Provide Team Incentives				
High-Moderate-Low	Bulk Buy Specials				
High-Moderate-Low	Collect All Prospect Details				
High-Moderate-Low	Company Profile				
High-Moderate-Low	Gimmick With Direct Mail				
High-Moderate-Low	Offer Exclusivity				
High-Moderate-Low	Set Sales Targets				
	Number of Transactions				
High-Moderate-Low	Better Service/Make Your Customers Feel Special				
High-Moderate-Low	Under Promise & Over Deliver				
High-Moderate-Low	Deliver Consistently & Reliably				
High-Moderate-Low	Keep In Regular Contact				
High-Moderate-Low	Timetable Of Communication				
High-Moderate-Low	Inform Customers Of Your Entire Range				
High-Moderate-Low	Product Of The Week				
High-Moderate-Low	Ask Them To Come Back				
High-Moderate-Low	Increase Your Range				
High-Moderate-Low	Increase Product Obsolescence/Upgrades				
High-Moderate-Low	Always Have Stock				
High-Moderate-Low	Offer Service Contracts				

Priority	Task	Individual Responsible	Investment	Start Date	Complete Date
High-Moderate-Low	Offer Free Trials				
High-Moderate-Low	Keep Clients Vital Information				
High-Moderate-Low	Send Out A Newsletter				
High-Moderate-Low	Run A Frequent Buyers Program/VIP Card				
High-Moderate-Low	Collect A Database				
High-Moderate-Low	Give Out Key Rings				
High-Moderate-Low	Pre-Sell Or Take Pre-Payments				
High-Moderate-Low	Contracts				
High-Moderate-Low	Till Further Notice Deals				
High-Moderate-Low	Plan Future Purchases				
High-Moderate-Low	Offer On Next Purchase				
High-Moderate-Low	Reminder System				
High-Moderate-Low	Accept Trade-Ins				
High-Moderate-Low	Increase Credit Levels				
High-Moderate-Low	Target Likely Repeaters				
High-Moderate-Low	Post Purchase Reassurance				
High-Moderate-Low	Suggest Alternative Uses				
High-Moderate-Low	Special Occasion Cards				
High-Moderate-Low	Direct Mail Regular Offers				
High-Moderate-Low	Follow Up & Follow Up Again				
High-Moderate-Low	Telemarket				

HOW TO CREATE AND DOMINATE YOUR NICHE

Priority	Task	Individual Responsible	Investment	Start Date	Complete Date
High-Moderate-Low	Run Contests				
High-Moderate-Low	Past Customer Events				
High-Moderate-Low	Closed Door Sales				
High-Moderate-Low	Fax Sales				
High-Moderate-Low	Named Promotional Gifts				
High-Moderate-Low	Information Nights				
High-Moderate-Low	Free Upgrades				
High-Moderate-Low	Socialize With Customers				
High-Moderate-Low	Labels & Stickers				
High-Moderate-Low	Catalogues				
High-Moderate-Low	Co-Operative Promotions				
High-Moderate-Low	Rent/Sell Your Database				
High-Moderate-Low	Clean Up Your Database				
High-Moderate-Low	Keep Good Data On Clients				
High-Moderate-Low	Train Your Team				
High-Moderate-Low	Offer A Shareholding In Your Company				
High-Moderate-Low	Sell More Consumables				
	Average Dollar Sale				
High-Moderate-Low	Increase Your Prices				
High-Moderate-Low	Up Sell				
High-Moderate-Low	Cross Or Add On Sell				

Priority	Task	Individual Responsible	Investment	Start Date	Complete Date
High-Moderate-Low	Down Sell				
High-Moderate-Low	Use A Checklist				
High-Moderate-Low	Use A Questionnaire				
High-Moderate-Low	Allow Payment Terms / Finance				
High-Moderate-Low	Carry Exclusive Lines				
High-Moderate-Low	Rearrange Store Layout / Merchandising				
High-Moderate-Low	Point Of Sale Material				
High-Moderate-Low	Impulse Buys				
High-Moderate-Low	Sell With An Either/Or Question				
High-Moderate-Low	Create Package Deals				
High-Moderate-Low	Create Bulk Buy Deals				
High-Moderate-Low	Allow Debit Cards, Cheques & Credit Cards				
High-Moderate-Low	Make Sure Clients Know Your Full Product & Service List				
High-Moderate-Low	Gift With SXX Purchase				
High-Moderate-Low	Charge Consulting Fees				
High-Moderate-Low	Sell Service Contracts				
High-Moderate-Low	Sell Extra Warranty/Insurance				
High-Moderate-Low	Train Your Team				
High-Moderate-Low	Use Sales Scripts				
High-Moderate-Low	Train Your Customers				
High-Moderate-Low	Create A Quality Image				

Priority	Task	Individual Responsible	Investment	Start Date	Complete Date
High-Moderate-Low	Only Service "A" Grade Customers				
High-Moderate-Low	Allow Trade-Ins/Trade-Ups				
High-Moderate-Low	Offer Home Delivery				
High-Moderate-Low	Charge For Delivery/Mail & Packaging				
High-Moderate-Low	Build Rapport/Treat As Special				
High-Moderate-Low	Set An Average Dollar Sale Goal				
High-Moderate-Low	Customer Incentives For Bigger Purchases				
High-Moderate-Low	Measure The Average S$ Sale				
High-Moderate-Low	Team Incentives For Bigger Sales				
High-Moderate-Low	Stop Discounting				
High-Moderate-Low	Add Value				
High-Moderate-Low	Give Away Perceived Value				
High-Moderate-Low	In Store Promotions				
High-Moderate-Low	Red Light Specials				
High-Moderate-Low	Educate On Value, Not Price				
High-Moderate-Low	Ask People To Buy Some More				
High-Moderate-Low	4 For The Price Of 3 Offers				
High-Moderate-Low	Buy One Get One Free Offers				
High-Moderate-Low	In Store Video Promotions				
High-Moderate-Low	Store, Team & Vehicle Appearance				
High-Moderate-Low	Suggest Most Expensive First				

Priority	Task	Individual Responsible	Investment	Start Date	Complete Date
High-Moderate-Low	Provide A Shopping List				
High-Moderate-Low	Have A Minimum $$ Order Amount				
High-Moderate-Low	Allow Lay-Away				

ABOUT THE AUTHOR

John Millar is the Managing Director, Senior Business Coach Trainer and Consultant with More Profit Less Time Pty Ltd and CEO-ONDEMAND. Along with his many other business interests, John is proud to have been an associate of the most successful coaching team in the world.

He is recognized as a global leader and has been benchmarked against over 1,300 colleagues in 31 countries. John has over 25 years of hands-on ownership, management, coaching, and entrepreneurial experience in a broad range of industry sectors, including retail, wholesale, import, export, IT, trades and trade services, automotive, primary production, food services, transport, manufacturing, mining, professional services, the fitness industry, and more.

He has extensive experience developing and providing training for small to medium-sized companies and a variety of publicly listed corporate companies. John is an accomplished and talented public and professional speaker. He has been a mentor working with sales/management activities for businesses with a turnover under $100,000 per annum, over $100 million turnover, and everything in between, with great success.

John currently works with business owners and their teams across Australia and has a "Whatever it takes" attitude that has enabled him to help his clients grow their business profits by up to 800%.

If you are ready to be coached by one of the best in the business, register at:

www.ceo-ondemand.com.au

Make sure to visit www.moreprofitlesstime.com for the new online Management Development Program: The Business Essentials Series.

CEOONDEMAND

ACCLAIM FOR JOHN MILLAR'S

Business Coaching and Training in their own words…

"Without John Millar as my Business Coach I wouldn't have a business today."—Grant Jennings Managing Director, Jigsaw Projects

"Taking the decision to be coached and trained by John Millar was carefully considered after experiencing those who over promised and under delivered. I am pleased to say the content of his courses are the tools we all need to master as business owners. His delivery is engaging, thought provoking and empowering and after every session l came away re-energised. John always makes himself available for business building advice both via Skype and face to face beyond the scope of delivery. With his extensive personal experience in building small businesses, he knows and understands what it takes to establish and grow a business.I have no hesitation endorsing John Millar as an educator and business coach and the bonus is he is a very nice person."— Anne Lederman Managing Director FB Salons"

Johns training with my management team was excellent, it was very different from the business coaching and support I have had in the past. John was clear, thoughtful and he addressed the issues we needed to cover without us even knowing they were being addressed! His follow up has been fantastic and exactly what I needed. I would recommend John and his team to anyone looking at getting some business coaching and training done" —Wendy Crawford, Peopleworx

"In my dealings with John as our business coach, I have found him to be a motivated and insightful agent of positive change. He is able to burrow down to the root cause of issues and introduce effective forms of measurement. John then identifies and implements practical solutions and is there to provide the gentle persuasion required to ensure that results are achieved." —Mark Felton, Lindale Insurances

"You have coached and trained us so well throughout the year that we are now used to & find it easy to prepare a 90 day plan, then breaks it down to actionable bite size pieces. Planning in business & personal life certainly is important. It allows us to identify the important things & the bigger picture. Thank you for your support & guidance throughout the year. And not to mention your insight, external perspective to review & assist our business moving forward." —Linda Turner, Director Roy A McDonald Certified Practicing Accountants

"If you want to achieve sales results you never thought were possible and give yourself a competitive edge my strong suggestion is to engage John services and listen closely to what John has to say, during the time I was trained by John I was one of eight sales consultants in a national business for 10 out of the 13 months I lead the sales tally and in 1 quarter I generated three times the revenue of the national sales force combined. Johns training and experience was well worth the investment and paid big dividends. Thanks John." —Julian Fadini, Bellvue Capital

"John is a very enthusiastic trainer and business coach, he is very passionate about getting business owners and their team where they need to be. He goes the extra mile to keep ahead of the latest developments which he then uses to benefit his clients." —Darren Reddy CPA

"I have been to a few seminars and heard John speak numerous times about sales, marketing and business. He is a very knowledgeable and extremely enthusiastic business coach in all his interactions and I would recommend him to all business owners who need a sales and marketing boost!" —Andrew Heath, Managing Director, Fresh Living Group

"I worked with John Millar and found his business knowledge, passion and innovation to be inspiring.

He has always been able to set (and achieve) strategic long and short-term goals both for himself and his clients without losing that personal connection he builds with everyone he meets. He has been and I believe will continue to be a strong mentor and trainer for anyone wanting to take that next step in their business." —Bree Webster, Online Marketing Guru

"Massive Action Day" – what an understatement, John Millar's 4 hour frenzy challenged me to seriously review areas of my business I would not have gone to …. In this way, the process identified incongruence's in my mind, my business and my modus operandi. It's created a paradigm shift. Thanks John, the road map just got a whole lot clearer. Your friendship and insights since 2003 have been a gift to my business and I." —Andrew Reay, Counsellor, Hypnotherapist and Counsellor, Thinkshift Transformations

"John Millar is not your usual Business coach or trainer; he gets involved with you and your business and provides hands on help to make sure you follow through on his advice. He is highly motivated to help his clients and his personal guarantee certainly shows this. He has now transposed his thoughts, advice and love of good business onto a series of DVD's in his business venture – More Profit Less Time. This has excellent tips and advice for anyone either starting out or already in business. I highly recommend John to any business owner who wants to run a business and not a j.o.b.!" —Darren Cassidy, Managing Director HR2U

"I and many of my Business Partners and colleagues have worked with John since 2010 as our business oath, trainer and motivator and found him to be an extremely motivational person to assist us achieve our business goals. This company and its products allows for John's skill set to be accessed by a wider number of potential clients. His very professional DVD series is extremely good value for money and is easily accessible for all of us who are time poor. If you are looking to maximise your and your business's results and to start achieving your goals and dreams, contact John; you won't look back!!" —Mark Cleland, Mortgage Choice

"John develops real relationships with the people he comes into contact with. He is passionate about what he does. His DVD and group training series, is full of good ideas and process to make your business better. Knowing what to do and actually doing it are two different things. John is excellent at helping you get things done." —Carey Rudd, Sales Director, Online Knowledge

"I have known John since 2004 and found him to be extremely knowledgably in both Sales and Business systems as a business coach without peer. John has provided me with business advice as well as personal coaching over the years, helping me with the running of my organisation. I'm impressed with John's DVD series where he has condensed a lot of the information in an easy to follow format that any business owner can use immediately. I wish he had released these DVDs earlier, as they are a goldmine of information, and practical how to that allow anyone to increase the profit in their business and get back valuable wasted time." —Steve Psaradellis, Managing Director, TEBA

"John's DVD and workbook delivery of his no-nonsense advice provides a low-cost option for those business owners looking to set and achieve goals that will increase profit. I found the conversational style of the DVD's easy to follow, whilst the requirement to pause the DVD and write down some action points ensured a level of commitment to the advice being provided." —Mark Felton, Lindale Insurances

"I only met John briefly at a BNI meeting and knew instantly i need to hire him for my business as my business coach. His attitude towards work and how to improve my cash line had an instant effect on before, even before I finally hired him on an official basis. I found myself thinking "what would John do" and this was only after just meeting him. I cannot see my business expend and give me "More Profit Less Time" without John's expert direction and training. If you want to succeed in business life, you need John Millar, without him you're just kidding yourself " — Leslie Cachia, Managing Director, Letac Drafting

"I can highly recommend John Millar to any business owner who wants to grow his business. When I hear very positive feedback from colleagues who are skeptics by nature about John's ability and skills, I know John will help all those he comes in contact with. John comes with a selfless nature and the willingness to work inside a client's business to make it succeed. Rare indeed!" —Darren Cassidy, Managing Director, HR2U"I first met John Millar in mid-2010 and have always found him to be of an honest and generous character that engenders an easy association with him. I love how easy he is to listen to and how passionate he is about his work and topics. John demonstrates a love for life and his work and I have no hesitation in recommending his services." —Kathie M Thomas, Managing Director, VA

"I have listened to John speak on a number of occasions and find him a very knowledgeable speaker with a passion for what he does. I have also interacted with a number of his clients and they all tell me that he helps them achieve results in their business. If you are looking for business help John is a person you can trust." —Carey Rudd, Sales Director, Online Knowledge

"John knows his stuff, he knows how the get results, John has so many great ideas in building a business and helping business owners work less and make more money. John has released a DVD set on doing just that. I have watched the 1st one and it was great, very informative and easy to understand, I happily recommend John to anyone in need of help and guidance" —Frank Eramo, Proprietor, Dynotune

"I have known John only for a short time, however the impact that he has had on me, not just my business has helped me to visualise opportunities that I began to doubt my ability to realise. He is encouraging and at the same time challenging so that he can/you can, begin to see how to maximise the business potential, John calls it being an unreasonable friend, I call it being a mate. If you have any questions about the direction of your business, if you want to seem your bottom line improve not just turnover but real profit, if you want a person who will work with you then I strongly recommend that you engage him at your earliest convenience. John is the best thing that has happened to my business. I could tell you about the way he is on track to make

1/2 a million for me on his contacts alone, but that actually sells him short, he has become like my partner in business, and cares about my success as if it was his own, we will flourish because I took the step to employ his training to help me grow. If you get a chance to get him training you, don't wait like I did, get in as quickly as possible, his time is your business and if like me your business is to make money, then every day you don't have him on retainer you lose money." —Russell Summers, Managing Director, The Give Life Centre

"It's usually easy to be mediocre in business but it's impossible when you have John Millar training you. He has been my right hand since 2003!" —David Manser, CFO, Hydrosteer

"I now have a commercial, profitable business and now it's my choice when I work IN my business and when I work ON it and have had john helping me in business since 1988. I can't imagine not having John as a part of our business." —David Wall, Director, D&K Transport

"The work John has done since 2008 coaching and training our marketing team, administration and finance teams, buyers, store managers and staff nationally have been fantastic." —Ross Sudano, Director, Anaconda Adventure Stores

"John is a creative, professional, practical and committed business coach and trainer. His approach since we first met him in 1994 to working with a client team through the application of useful tools, information and anecdotes along with his easy going & easy to understand delivery sets him apart from

other business coaches that I have used in the past."
—Anthony Beasley, Director, The Astra Group

"I have worked with John Millar for the since 2004 and I didn't think it was possible to achieve what we have achieved together. His business coaching, training and services just get better and better!" — Terrance Chong, Managing Director, Echo Graphics and Printing

"John's business coaching, training and support has transformed our business across Australia and New Zealand since 2008."—rose vis, managing director, VIP Australia

"We first met John in 2005, he is AMAZING at sales, marketing, operations, logistics, finance training and so much more. Since engaging John as our business coach our business has exploded, our team are happy, our clients are raving about us and my husband and I now take at least 12 weeks holidays a year, EVERY year." —Shirley Du, Director, Goldline Technology

"It's the no nonsense results driven business coaching and training focus John bought to the table that had such a massive effect on our business." — David Runkel, Director, Tracomp Fabrication and Steel

"We started working with John in early 2010, within 90 days of working with and being trained by John Millar we had the biggest and most profitable month in our 15 year history. That's impressive." —Hugh Gilchrist, Managing Director, Australian Moulding Company

"If you don't have John as your business trainer you aren't meeting your business potential." —Don Robertson, Director, Medallion Electrical Services

Thank You!

www.ingramcontent.com/pod-product-compliance
Lightning Source LLC
Chambersburg PA
CBHW060356190526
45169CB00002B/623